D1518880

BIG BEASTS
Eagle

Stephanie Turnbull

Published by Smart Apple Media
P.O. Box 1329
Mankato, MN 56002

Printed in the United States of America,
at Corporate Graphics in North Mankato, Minnesota.

Designed by Hel James
Edited by Mary-Jane Wilkins

Library of Congress Cataloging-in-Publication Data

Turnbull, Stephanie.
 Eagle / Steph Turnbull.
   p. cm. -- (Big beasts)
 Includes index.
 Summary: "An introduction on eagles, the big beasts in the sky.
Describes how eagles fly, find food, communicate, and care for
their young. Also mentions the different kinds of eagles and their
differences"--Provided by publisher.
 ISBN 978-1-59920-832-9 (hardcover, library bound)
 1. Eagles--Juvenile literature. I. Title.
 QL696.F32T866 2013
 598.9'42--dc23
                       2012004111

Photo acknowledgements
l = left, r = right; t = top, b = bottom, c = center
page 1 withGod/Shutterstock; 3 Tom Brakefield/Thinkstock;
4 Chris Humphries/Shutterstock; 6 abxyz/Shutterstock;
7t iStockphoto/Thinkstock, b worldswildlifewonders/Shutterstock;
9 Michal Ninger/Shutterstock; 10t Gregory Johnston/Shutterstock,
bl Design Pics/Thinkstock, r James DeBoer/Shutterstock;
12 iStockphoto/Thinkstock; 13 visceralimage/Shutterstock;
14 peter_krejzl/Shutterstock; 15 Josh Anon/Shutterstock; Jeff
Banke/Shutterstock; 17 Matt Ragen/Shutterstock; 18 Stockbyte/
Thinkstock; 19 iStockphoto/Thinkstock; 20 jo Crebbin/
Shutterstock; 21 Alucard2100/Shutterstock; 22t Catalin Petolea/
Shutterstock, c iStockphoto/Thinkstock, b rimira/Shutterstock;
23t Valery Kraynov/Shutterstock, b Tatiana Popova/Shutterstock
Cover Ryan McVay/Thinkstock

DAD0503
042012
9 8 7 6 5 4 3 2 1

Contents

Eagles are
enormous!

3

Huge Hunters

Eagles are powerful,
fierce birds of prey.

They glide through the
air on long, wide wings,
searching for animals to eat.

Layers of large, waterproof
feathers keep them warm.

5

Lots of Eagles

Here are some of the **biggest** eagles.

Steller's sea eagles live in Russia and Japan. They have enormous beaks.

Philippine eagles are the world's rarest birds of prey.

Harpy eagles swoop through Central and South American forests.

7

Eagle Eyes

Eagles have amazing eyesight.

They can spot a fish far below in the sea, or spy a rabbit way off in the grass.

They even have see-through eyelids, so they don't miss anything when they blink!

Dinner Time!

Eagles eat
any food they
can find.

This may be fish, snakes, and small birds, or even monkeys, deer, or sloths.

They swoop down faster than a speeding car and grab prey in their long talons.

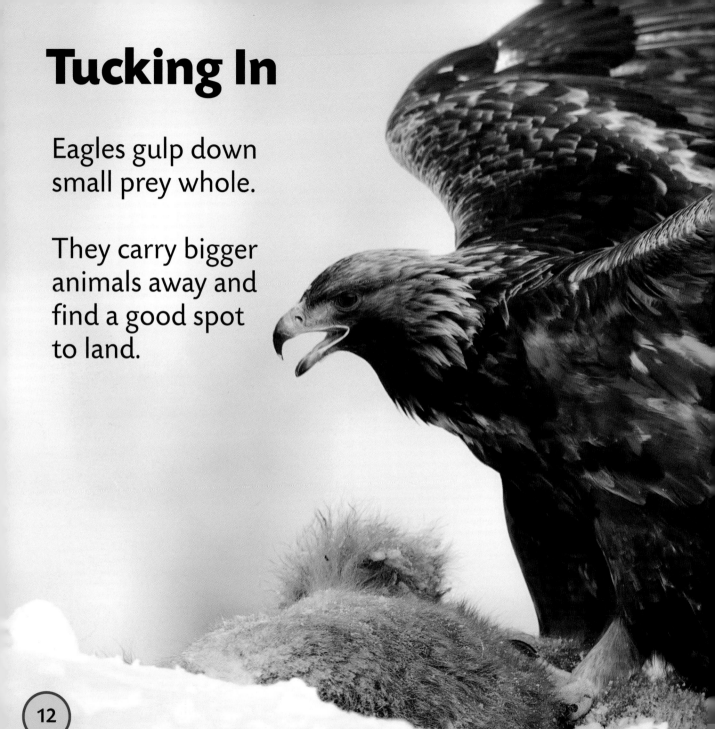

Tucking In

Eagles gulp down small prey whole.

They carry bigger animals away and find a good spot to land.

Their razor-sharp, hooked beak is perfect for ripping off chunks of flesh.

Amazing Acrobats

Eagles are fast, graceful fliers.
They dive and loop to show off
to other eagles.

Sometimes two eagles lock talons and spiral down... down...

...then fly apart before they hit the ground.

Enormous Nests

Eagle pairs build huge nests in trees and other high places.

The female lays eggs in the nest.
Both eagles take turns to sit on the
eggs to keep them safe and warm.

Fluffy Chicks

Newly-hatched baby eagles are called eaglets.

Eaglets wait for their parents to bring scraps of meat to eat. They quickly grow bigger and stronger.

Growing Up

Soon eaglets grow proper feathers. Now they can learn to fly.

They take short flights
at first. It isn't easy!

This young bald eagle is brown.
In a few years it will grow adult feathers.

BIG Facts

The biggest eagles can spread their wings wider than you and a friend laid end to end.

An eagle's nest is bigger than your bed.

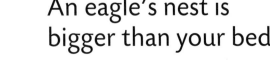

Eagles can weigh
more than four cats.

Some eagles have legs
as thick as your wrist.

Useful Words

bird of prey
A fierce bird that hunts and eats other birds and animals, called prey.

rare
Not very common. There are not many Philippine eagles today, so they are rare.

talon
A long, sharp claw. Eagles have four strong talons on each foot for grabbing and carrying prey.

Index

Web Link
Go to this website for bald eagle facts, photos and a video:
http://kids.nationalgeographic.com/kids/animals/creaturefeature/baldeagle